I WISH
I HAD A
PIRATE
HAT

FOR SAM

JANETTA OTTER-BARRY BOOKS

Text copyright © Roger Stevens 2015
Illustrations copyright © Lorna Scobie 2015
The right of Roger Stevens to be identified as the author of this work
has been asserted by him in accordance with the Copyright,
Designs and Patents Act, 1988 (United Kingdom).

First published in Great Britain and in the USA in 2015 by
Frances Lincoln Children's Books, 74–77 White Lion Street,
London N1 9PF
www.franceslincoln.com

A catalogue record for this book is available from the British Library.

ISBN 978-1-84780-618-5

Printed and bound by CPI Group (UK) Ltd, Croydon, CR0 4YY

9 8 7 6 5 4 3 2 1

For Stanley

I WISH
I HAD A
PIRATE
HAT

Roger Stevens.

Poems by
ROGER STEVENS

Drawings by
LORNA SCOBIE

Frances Lincoln
Children's Books

Oct '17

CONTENTS

The Pirate Map

In a cave, in the cliffs
we found a map
of a sea that was dangerous
and grey

On the sea was an island
of trees and sand
and the island
was far, far away

And on the island
was drawn an X
where we had to dig
in the grass

And beneath the X
there was a chest
of oak planks
bound with brass

So we pulled up the chest
and opened the lid
and we gasped and groaned
in dismay

For in the chest
there was a map
of a sea that was dangerous
and grey

I Wish I Had a Pirate Hat

I wish I had
a pirate hat
a pirate hat, a pirate hat
I wish I had a pirate hat
like my mate Jack's
pirate hat

So I said to Jack
let's swap your hat,
pirate hat, pirate hat
I said to Jack, I'll swap your hat
swap your hat
for a football

So now I have
a pirate hat
a pirate hat, a pirate hat
Now I have a pirate hat
'cos I gave Jack
my football

But the sun is out
in the park
in the park, in the park
and my mates are playing
in the park
and I wish I had
a football

Good Pirate, Bad Pirate

I am a good pirate because
I give my parrot peanuts

I am a bad pirate because
I sink enemy ships and steal their treasure

I am a good pirate because
I give half of everything I steal to the poor

I am a bad pirate because
I make my captives walk the plank

I am a good pirate because
I always say sorry afterwards

I am a bad pirate because
I bury my treasure in a deep hole on a deserted island

I am a good pirate because
I draw a treasure map that makes it easy to find

I am a bad pirate because
I tie prisoners to the mast

I am a good pirate because
I read them bedtime stories

When Space Creatures Catch a Cold

When space creatures catch a cold
They sneeze like we do
But their sneezes can be rather strange
I'll show you just a few

A space dog sneezes
Just like a dog on Earth
atishoo

But a space worm goes
beep beep

A space bug goes
mmmmmmmmmeeeeeeeeCHOO!

And a space hopper goes
tishoo BONK tishoo BONK tishoo BONK

But scariest of all is the space monster
who goes

KABOOMKA

Big Red Pedal Car

I sat in the big red pedal car
and pushed the pedals
The pedals were stiff
and the car moved slowly
Very very
S l o w l y

It was hard work
and although for a moment
I imagined I was in a sleek red racing car
F a s t and **LOUD**
roaring around the racetrack

It was only
a big red pedal car
with stiff pedals
moving very slowly

so I parked the car
and ran

Is the Moon Made of Cheese?

Grandpa said,
"The moon
is made of cheese."

And so I said to Grandpa,
"If the moon is made of cheese
and cheese is made from milk
and milk comes from cows…
where are the cows?

Where are the giant space cows
who made the milk
that made the cheese
that made the moon?"

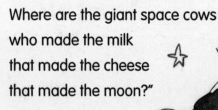

And Grandpa
tapped his nose
and winked and said,
"It's a secret."

Moon

Moon
With your serious face

Moon
Are you watching the Earth
Spinning in space?

Moon
Are you watching the stars twinkling?

Moon
What you are thinking?

A Poem to Make You Jump

This poem will make you jump.
Not jump like a kangaroo
or a flea on your knee
jumping into your tea
or a bee with a sneeze.
Atishoo!

This poem will make you jump
like the moan of a ghost in the park
or an owl in the trees,
like the jangle of keys
that you hear in the door in the dark.

So… imagine it's dark,
imagine it's night
and the moon is a silvery blue,
and you're wondering how
can a poem make you jump?

Well…

be very quiet…

listen… and…

BOO!

Puppy in the Woods

Sam and Grandad
were walking in the woods.
Sam said, "Grandad, I feel sad."
So Grandad asked Sam,
"Why are you feeling sad?"
Sam said, "I don't know."

Sam and Grandad
were walking in the woods
and they met a puppy called Mo.
The puppy jumped and ran around
and his tail wagged and wagged
to and fro like an excited flag
and the puppy chased Sam
and Sam was shrieking and
laughing and giggling.

Sam and Grandad
were walking through the woods
and Sam said, "Grandad,
Do you know what?
I'm not feeling sad any more."

Things I Found on the Beach

by Sam Decie (aged 5)

A pebble
An empty pot
A sea scorpion
A donkey
An eyeball
A whole pirate ship
Five aliens
A time machine
Grandad's hair
Grandad's glasses
Grannie's necklace
And a magic crystal

Tyrannosaurus Rex

Tyrannosaurus Rex
with your big sharp teeth
and tiny little arms

How does it feel
to have no friends
because you are so scary?

I have to say
I'm very pleased
that you're not real

Being Sad

When I'm meeting Milly in the park
And Milly doesn't show

When I ask my best friend for a crisp
And my best friend says no

When I bite into a juicy plum
And the middle has gone bad

Even writing this poem
Is making me feel sad

My Mates and Me

(for James Carter)

I've got a friend
His name is James
He loves to play
Rhyming games

I've got a pal
His name is Brian
He makes words roar
Just like a lion

I have a chum
Her name is Jan
She hides poems
In the watering can

I have a mate
Her name is Liz
She makes words
Bubble and fizz

And when my friends
Come round to play
Our poems chase
The clouds away

Grey Cloud

A rain cloud is grey
and when it rains
you have to play
indoors

But when it rains
flowers grow
and the caterpillars come
and chew the new green leaves

And the caterpillars become butterflies
Red Admirals
Cabbage Whites
Chalk Hill Blues
Meadow Browns
Clouded Yellows
Painted Ladies

There are bright butterfly colours
everywhere
and all because
the clouds are grey

Running in the Park

I love running in the park
Running, running
Looking in the fish pond
Waving at the shark
Running, running
Listening to the bees
Running, running
I can smell smoke
There's the dragon
Diving from the sky
And I'm running, running
And I can fly
Come on, Grandad
Don't be slow
Look how fast I can go!
Running through the park
That's what I like best
But now I've got to stop

So that Grandad can rest.

I Can't Catch You

Squirrel scampering
I can't catch you
as quick as a wriggle
in the tree so high

Pigeon pecking
I can't catch you
as quick as an acrobat
flying in the sky

Dragonfly darting
I can't catch you
as quick as a blink
crossing the brook

Pond-skater skimming
I can't catch you
as quick as a scribble
in a green notebook

A Great Place To Be

Five buzzing bees
collecting pollen from the flowers
zipping and humming
I could watch them for hours.

Four tiny butterflies
two blue, two white
chasing one another
through the grassy sunlight.

Three green grasshoppers
if you look very closely
hiding in the grass
then pinging so high.

Two birds flying
in loops and circles
interweaving patterns
in the bright blue sky.

And in this summer field
one little me
standing and watching.
What a great place to be!

Fly and Bee

*It might be fun to make up a little tune
and a dance to go with the humming
and buzzing part of the poem.*

Fly and bee
bee and fly
do a little dance
where the grass grows high

hmmmm   hmmmm
buzzzz   buzzzz

Bee and fly
fly and bee
sing a little song
in harmony

hmmmm   buzzzz
buzzzz   hmmmm

Birds Flying South

More birds than I can count at once
Whirl and swirl in the sky
They are flying south to find the sun
I wave and say goodbye

Their journey is a thousand miles
They travel night and day
How do they know where they have to go?
And how do they find their way?

Jet Plane

Arms out wide
Either side
Warm up

brmbrmbrmbrmbrmbrm

Run
Faster
Take off

yeeeeeeeeeeahhhhowwww

Racing past
Leaning, curving
Swooping

eeeeeeeeyyyyyyyOWWwwwwwwoooooo

JET PLANE

Beanstalk

At half past ten
when everyone
puts their books away
and lines up for their fruit
Sam and I have to check the beanstalk.

We planted ten beans
but only one grew,
and it grew and grew
and now it's touching the ceiling.
Sam says beans are strong
and it will probably push a hole in the ceiling
and go right through the roof.

We have to water it every day
and we talk to it too.
Because Sam says plants like being talked to.
Sam's reading it a story,
Jack and the Beanstalk.
"I wonder," says Sam, "if it will grow up to the sky
and if we climb it we'll find a chicken who lays
a golden egg."

"Do you know what?" I say,
"I think it will grow that tall."
"Wow!" says Sam. "When we get the golden egg,
shall we sell it for a million pounds?"
"You're forgetting something," I say.
"What's that?"
"There won't only be a golden egg.
There will also be
a big, scary giant!"

It's Not Fair

The rain seems to know
when it's playtime

The sun shines from nine until ten

Then a cloud appears
and at playtime it rains

After playtime
the sun's out again

Miss Moss Knows Everything

Who knows everything?
Miss Moss, our teacher, does.

What follows a dog wherever he goes?
What does a polite mouse say?
Why do bees hum as they work in the sun?

Who knows everything?
Miss Moss, our teacher, does.

A tail follows a dog around.
A mouse says cheese and thank you.
Bees always hum because they don't know the words.

Who knows everything?
Miss Moss, our teacher, does.

Why do spiders live in cupboards?
Why do coconuts have hair?
Why won't Billy Stokes share?

Who knows everything?
Our teacher does.
That's who.

The Things Billy Said He Found Down the Back of a Chair

A pound coin

A spotty sock

A small teddy bear

A Liverpool pencil sharpener

An Angry Birds fridge magnet

A chocolate eclair

A trumpet

A telescope

A yellow plastic flower

A skateboard

A hippopotamus

The Eiffel Tower

A Tyrannosaurus Rex

And a cheese and onion toastie

"Is that true?" Miss Moss asked.

Billy said,

"Well…

mostly…"

Pictures of Dragons

We made pictures of dragons
We painted on the big paper sheets
with dragon colours
green scales paint
and big splodges of red fire paint
and when it was dry
we drew the dragon on top
in bold black lines

Then we talked about our dragons
flying through the dark clouds
breathing fire
Dylan's dragon was fantastic
It looked angry and wild
and everyone said
it was the most terrible and terrifying dragon of all
because it had two tails
and two heads

I wonder if you could draw a picture of a
more terrifying dragon than these?

47

The Poetry Shed

for Mile Oak School

In the playground
is a Poetry Shed
and we all love
the Poetry Shed.

Heddie and Jake
and Me and Fred
love reading poems
in the Poetry Shed.

It's a shed in the playground
painted red
and big gold letters say
Poetry Shed.

I read poems to Granny
and poems in bed
but my best place to read
is the Poetry Shed.

The Visiting Poet

We had a visiting poet
He was really funny
He told us a poem
about pond dipping
and as he was reaching for a frog
with his net
he fell off his chair
and we laughed and laughed

So I drew a picture
of the visiting poet
and he loved my picture
even though his head
did look a bit
like a turnip

The Letter B

Miss Moss said,
"Tell me, tell me please,
an animal or creature
beginning with B."

Ben said, "Beetle."
And Bridie said, "Bear."
Bella said, "Bird."
And Billy said, "Chair."

Miss Moss said, "Billy,
can't you see?
A chair's not an animal
beginning with B."

"Well," said Billy,
"I could have said Bat.
Or Badger, or Bunny
or something like that.

I could have said Butterfly
but, just for a dare,
I put up my hand
and called out Chair."

Making Words

I wish I could
spill butter

I wish I could
spall bitter

I wish I could
spell batter

I wish I could
spell better

The Two-Syllable Club

My name's Sammy.
Teacher says
I am in the two-syllable club
with Summer
and Donna
and Sarah.

I'm glad I'm not in the five-syllable club
like Anastasia.

No one else has five syllables.
It must be very lonely there.

Fairy Dust

Our teacher sprinkles fairy dust
She keeps it in a jar
She gathers it by moonlight
It comes down from a star

She sprinkles it on naughty boys
It stops them being silly
And helps them work, and sit up straight
But it doesn't work on Billy

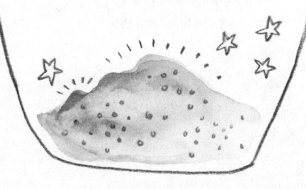

What Am I?

When you wake up you see me
and sigh
At lunchtime you see me
and grin
At three o'clock you see me
and cheer

I have a face
but no eyes
I have hands
but no fingers

Have you guessed me yet?
Then it's about time you did.

A clock

Big Numbers

One for the ladybird
in her coat of black and red

Ten for the centipedes
living in the shed

Fifty for the pea bugs
underneath the mat

One hundred for the flies
flying round the cowpat

One thousand for the worker ants
working on the ground

One million for the tiny creatures
living all around

Home Time

We line up in the corridor,
bump and shuffle,
push and squeeze,
shuffle and bump,
squeeze and push.

Miss Moss opens the door.
There's Granny on the playground
and lots of mums and dads.

I wave and Miss Moss calls my name.

Then I run on to the playground
and hug Granny
and me and my friends
are running and laughing,
jumping and shouting,
climbing the giant red dinosaur
and whooping and yelling
and laughing and running.

It's home time, home time
It's time to go
HOME!

HOME TIME

Billy Woke Up

On Monday
Billy woke up
Opened his eyes
And *guess what he saw!*
A tiger
Wearing a wig
And an elephant
Dancing a jig.

On Tuesday
Billy woke up
Opened his eyes
And *guess what he heard!*
Mum playing her trumpet
Dad playing his flute
They were playing a tune
Rooti tooti tooti toot.

On Wednesday
Billy woke up
Opened his cupboard
And *guess what he found!*

Half a doughnut
A bag of cashews
And a little white mouse
Having a snooze.

On Thursday
Billy woke up
He went to the bathroom
And *guess what he saw!*
Two ducks in the bath
Rehearsing a play
And a frog in a basin
Who wished him, "Good day."

On Friday
Billy woke up
And *guess what he did!*
He fell asleep again.
He dreamt he was eating
A gooseberry fool
And when he woke up
He was late for school.

My Special Big Blue Cup

My special cup
has my name on it.

It's a big cup.
It's a big blue cup.
It's a big blue plastic cup.
It's a big blue plastic cup full of apple juice

and if you drop it
it doesn't break,
it bounces.

But the juice spills out
all over the floor,
and Mum gets cross and says,

"Just be a bit more careful
when you hold your special cup."

And she gets the apple juice and says,
"Now, here's a little more."

It's a big cup.
It's a big blue cup.
It's a big blue plastic cup.
It's a big blue plastic cup full of apple juice
and it's got my name on it.

Chicken Soup

Hear the soup
Bubble

Smell the soup
Yum

See the soup
Cook

Touch the bowl
Hot

Taste the soup
Yuck!

**I don't like
chicken soup**

Shhh...

I know where Mum
hides her chocolate biscuits.

I'm not going to tell you
because it's a secret.

There were five in the packet
but now there are four.

I wonder if she'll notice
if I have just one more?

The Best Drink

I quite like Coke
and I quite like milk.
I quite like lemonade
as fizzy as can be.
I quite like milkshake,
I quite like chocolate,
I quite like orange
and I quite like tea.

But when I'm very thirsty,
very, very thirsty
like a camel in the desert,
as thirsty as can be.
Then I really like water,
smooth, cold water,
cool, clear water –
that's the drink for me.

Teatime with Little Rabbit

Hey, little rabbit
Would you like a little cuddle?
I can feel your tiny beating heart

Hey, little rabbit
Would you like a little snuggle
and a nibble on my raspberry tart?

Pussy Cat

Pussy Cat
Pussy Cat
That is your name

You came
Into our home
When you were quite young
A stray cat
A thin cat
Bedraggled and sad
And Mum said
You could stay

You soon settled in
And we called you Pussy Cat
Pussy Cat
Pussy Cat
I wonder why
We never gave you
A proper name?

Monsters

The Hoover Monster
Roaring and grumbling
Snarling and hissing
It's so
SCARY!

The lawnmower monster
Whirring and clanking
Clonking and whining
It's so

SCARY!

The dishwasher monster
Rattling and rocking
Rolling and shaking
It's so

SCARY!

It's so scary…
if you're
a dog
like
me.

Spider

I went into the bathroom
And what did I see?
A spider in the bath.
It was looking at me.

It said, Help me, help me,
help me, please!
I've got eight legs
and I've got eight knees.

But when I try to climb out
my eight legs slip.
Help me, help me,
I can't get a grip.

I went into the bathroom
and heard a shout.
There was a spider in the bath
so I pulled him out.

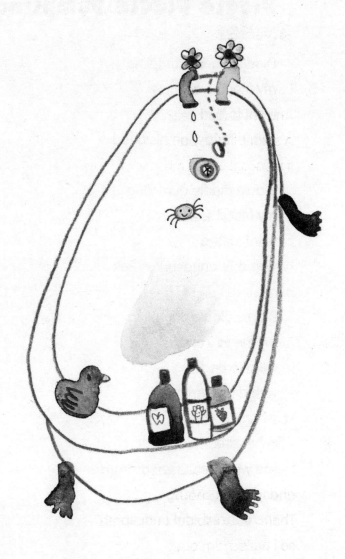

Diddle Diddle Dumpling

Diddle diddle dumpling
my friend Fred
went to bed
with a teapot on his head

Diddle diddle dumpling
my friend Tex
went to bed
with a Tyrannosaurus Rex

Diddle diddle dumpling
my friend Zena
went to bed
with a concertina

In her dreams
she was the Queen of France
and all night long
she danced and danced

Good Night, Mister Moon

Good night Mister Moon
Lighting the sky
Night time has come
Now it's just you and I

You sail like a ship
In an ocean of stars
Passing comets and satellites
Venus and Mars

Over lions in Africa
Crossing the seas
Above temples in India
And tall redwood trees

How far you have travelled
Spreading your light
And now you are here
In my window tonight

So, good night Mister Moon
Your silver moonbeams
Say goodbye to the day
As I drift off to dreams.

Roger Stevens has written lots of poetry books
and stories for children. Roger wanted to be a pirate
when he grew up but he decided to be a writer instead.
He lives in Brighton with his wife
and a very, very scary dog called Jasper.
He often goes down to the beach to search for treasure.
So far all he has found has been
pebbles, seaweed and a huge piece of
driftwood that looks like a pirate ship's anchor.
Roger also runs the award-winning children's poetry
website, The Poetry Zone, where you can send
Roger your own pirate poems.

www.poetryzone.co.uk

MORE POETRY FOR YOUNGER CHILDREN FROM FRANCES LINCOLN CHILDREN'S BOOKS

Hey Little Bug!
9781847801685

I'm a Little Alien!
9781847804815

Here Come the
Creatures!
9781847803672